OXFORD BOOKWORMS LIBRARY
Factfiles

Building a Better World

The United Nations Sustainable Development Goals

RACHEL BLADON

Level 2 (700 headwords)

Series Editor: Rachel Bladon
Acting Series Editor: Madeleine Burgess
Editors: Hannah Fish and Alyson Jones

OXFORD
UNIVERSITY PRESS

Great Clarendon Street, Oxford, OX2 6DP, United Kingdom

Oxford University Press is a department of the University of Oxford.
It furthers the University's objective of excellence in research, scholarship,
and education by publishing worldwide. Oxford is a registered trade
mark of Oxford University Press in the UK and in certain other countries

ISBN: 978 0 19 426798 4   Book
ISBN: 978 0 19 426795 3   Book and audio pack

For more information on the Oxford Bookworms Library,
visit www.oup.com/elt/gradedreaders
Printed in China

ACKNOWLEDGEMENTS

Cover image: Shutterstock avijit boari

Illustrations by: JiaJia Hamner/Advocate Art

*The publisher would like to thank the following for their permission to reproduce
photographs*: Alamy Alex Segre, Farah Abdi Warsameh/Associated Press,
Magdalena Bujak, Dmitry Shironosov, Lightfield Studios, Andre Penner/
Associated Press, ARphotography, Nature Picture Library, dpa Picture
Alliance; Getty FG Trade/E+, Westend61, David Freund/Photodisc,
commerceandculturestock, Daniele Badolato – Juventus FC, Thomas Koehler/
Photothek, Moment RF, Joe Petro/Icon Sportswire, Ross Helen/iStock, urbazon/
E+, Andrew Merry/Moment RF, Hill Street Studios, Central Press/Hulton
Archive, Stuart Fox/Gallo Images ROOTS Collection; Reuters Thomas Mukoya;
Shutterstock Owlie Productions, Jenson, WhiteJack, PradeepGaurs, Have a nice
day Photo, albertoudor, milatas, Media Lens King, BAZA Production, Jose Luis
Stephens, Carolina Jaramillo, Lumir Jurka Lumia, Rich Carey, Hari Mahidhar, nito,
Ruslan Shugushev, Galina Barskaya, luchschenF, fizkes, gopixa, Monkey Business
Images, 1981 Rustic Studio kan, StanislauV, Ralf Geithe
Sustainable Development Goal icons featured by arrangement with
the United Nations

The publisher wishes to thank Tom Le Seelleur for his expert help
in developing the content.

United Nations Sustainable Development Goals:
https://www.un.org/sustainabledevelopment/
The content of this publication has not been approved by the United Nations and
does not reflect the views of the United Nations or its officials or Member States.

CONTENTS

1   A plan for the future

Close your eyes and think of this:

The world is bright, and people are laughing and smiling. Life is good, and everyone has money, enough food to eat, and clean water to drink. Everyone is healthy, all children go to school, and all adults have work that pays well. Cities and towns are wonderful places. The land and oceans are clean and beautiful, and plants and animals are safe. There is no conflict in the world, and we have stopped climate change. We have everything!

It is a story, of course. But these things really are possible. Nobody needs to be hungry or poor, and we can stop climate change. We can build a better world for everyone and, in 2015, the United Nations (UN) made a plan for this.

The UN is one of the most important organizations in the world. There are 193 countries in the UN, and they all work together and try to find answers to the world's biggest problems. In 2015, these countries knew that they all had to make many changes, and they agreed on seventeen goals called the 'Sustainable Development Goals' or SDGs. The SDGs explain what we need to do to change our world and build a better future before 2030, and all the countries in the UN began making these important changes.

SUSTAINABLE DEVELOPMENT GALS

1 No poverty

2 No hunger

3 Good health

4 Good education

5 Equality for women and girls

6 Clean water

7 Sustainable energy

8 Good economies

9 Good work

10 Equality

11 A good place to live

12 Sustainable living

13 Stop climate change

14 Healthy oceans

15 Healthy land

16 No conflict

17 Working together

Each of the SDGs talk about a different problem in the world, like poverty or hunger. But not everyone is poor or hungry; many of the problems in the world are worse for some people than others. And they are worse in some countries of the world, too. These countries are often called 'developing countries', and many of them are in Africa, Asia, and Latin America. SDG 10 talks about this: it says that there must be equality for every person in every country, then the world will be a better, safer place for everyone.

All the SDGs explain how we can give everyone what they need in a sustainable way. When something is sustainable, it is safe for the future of the world. This is very important. If we do not make changes in a sustainable way, we will make new or bigger problems. For example, if we build thousands of new factories and farms to make more food and end hunger, there will be more pollution and climate change. So we must build a better world in a careful and sustainable way.

After the SDGs were made in 2015, a lot of good work happened across the world. But then, in 2020, millions of people got the terrible new disease Covid-19. Lots of people died, and many were ill or could not work or go to school. Countries had to spend a lot of money to keep people safe from the disease, and they could not pay for other things. So, since 2020, problems like hunger and poverty have not got better – they have got worse. 7.8% of people in the world were living in poverty in 2019. By 2021, that number was 9.1%. We need to work even harder for a better world because of Covid-19, and every one of us needs to help.

Perhaps you are thinking, 'How can *I* change the world? I'm just one person in a world of billions'. But

if everyone makes one small change in their lives, there are lots of small changes. And together, lots of small changes are very big!

When you tell other people, like your friends, about making changes, that also helps. Because perhaps when your friends hear about what you are doing, they will all make some changes, too. And if these people tell their friends, who all tell their friends, then there will be many more changes in the world. It is like dropping a stone in water. The stone only breaks the water for a second, but the circles move across the water and get bigger and bigger.

Each chapter in this book describes one or more of the SDGs. It explains why we need each goal, and gives examples of people or organizations that are working for change. Each chapter tells you how you can help, too.

2   No poverty

 There must be no poverty in the world.

The word *poverty* means 'not having enough money', and living in poverty is very hard. People who are poor often cannot pay for the things that are important for all of us. They cannot buy enough food, live in a safe home, or travel when they need to. For example, it can be difficult to get to school or see a doctor.

We say that someone is living in extreme poverty when they do not have more than $1.90 a day. Today, about 10% of people in the world – and 20% of children – are living in extreme poverty.

THINK

How much money do you usually spend in a day? What can you buy for $1.90?

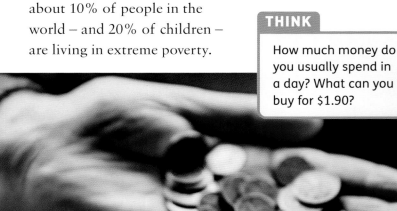

Why is it so difficult to escape from poverty?

1 This child is living in poverty. He does not get enough food or clean water.

2 He is very tired and cannot walk 5 kilometres to the nearest school.

3 He does not get an education, and he is not healthy because he is always hungry. He cannot get a job and has no money.

4 He marries and has a baby. The family has no money, and it is very difficult for them to buy food and clothes for the baby.

Selling cheap bicycles in Zambia

In Zambia, in Africa, many people live in small villages that are a long way from the nearest town. The people in these villages are often very poor, and it is difficult for them to go to town to find work or sell things.

Wyson Lungu decided to do something to help these people, and he started selling very cheap bicycles to them. People only pay a little money every month to buy a bicycle, and the bicycles are changing their lives.

One farmer from a village in Zambia bought one of Lungu's bicycles, and she uses it to carry milk from her cows to the nearest town. Before, she had to walk to the town, and the journey took a long time. Now, she can carry more milk on her bicycle, and the milk does not go bad because it arrives quickly – so, she is getting a lot more money for the milk.

Helping homeless people in Japan

In Ikebukuro, in Tokyo, an organization called Tenohasi is working with people who have nowhere to live. Often, these people are living in poverty, because they cannot find a job, have no help from friends or family, are ill, or have a disability.

When someone has no home, it is easy for them to feel alone and not know how to get help. But at Tenohasi, which began in 2003, helpers talk with these people and help them to find safe homes. They also give them hot meals and clean clothes and shoes, and people can get help with their health problems. In just one day, Tenohasi helpers can give hot meals to over 500 people who need them.

What can I do?

→ Do not sell or throw away clothes, shoes, books, or other things in your home when you do not want them any more. Give them to people who need them, or to shops that sell them to help others.

→ When you are in a supermarket, look for a food box for people who are living in poverty. Buy one or two things and put them in the box.

→ Give your time to help an organization that makes meals for people who are living in poverty.

→ Do you often spend money on something special, like a cup of coffee or going to the cinema? For one month, stop doing that thing. Save the money, and give it to an organization that helps people who are living in poverty.

3   No hunger

 Everyone must have enough food, every day.

We all need good food to be healthy, and there is enough food in the world for everyone. But more than 800 million people are hungry every day, and hunger is the biggest killer in the world. In 2021, 1,000 people died from hunger every hour. Most of the people who are hungry live in developing countries. In some countries in Africa, nearly 20% of people are hungry all the time.

Hunger is also a bigger problem for women and girls than for men and boys. Nearly 60% of hungry people are women and girls. This is because many women do not get a good education or job, so they do not have enough money to buy food. And, in some countries, women and girls have to eat last when a family does not have enough food.

THINK

What time is it now? How many people have died from hunger today?

Why is there so much hunger in the world?

Conflict

When there is fighting in a country, it can be difficult and dangerous to work and to travel. So, people often cannot grow as much food as usual, or take food to the people who need it.

Climate change

Because of climate change, some countries can have too much rain, or they have very hot, dry weather. When this happens, food cannot grow well there.

Poverty

Half the people in the world are very poor. They cannot buy food because they do not have enough money.

Hunger

Food waste

Across the world, about one-third of all food is thrown away every year. Sometimes, this is because people buy more food than they need. Or there can be a lot of food waste when people live in a hot country but they do not have places to keep food cold. So, after a short time, they have to throw food away.

More people

The number of people in the world grows by about 1% every year, so it gets more and more difficult to make enough food for everyone.

Drying food in India

In Maharashtra, in the west of India, it is very hot, so farmers often have to throw away fruit and vegetables before they can sell them. But some people there have started a new business making special dryers which can dry food very quickly. They pay women who live in the villages of Maharashtra to dry fruit and vegetables, which are then good to eat for up to six months.

Now, there is more food in Maharashtra, and the business is helping people in other ways, too. Poor farmers are now getting more money because they can sell *all* their fruit and vegetables. And the business is giving jobs to women who did not have jobs before.

Growing 'Green Super Rice' in China

Farmers cannot always grow enough rice for everyone because there are more and more people in the world every year. Also, there is a lot of extreme weather because of climate change, and this can destroy rice fields or make rice grow very slowly.

But people in China have worked hard to make a new rice called 'Green Super Rice' (GSR). GSR is very strong, and it still grows well when there is too much rain or when the weather is too dry. Farmers are now growing GSR in many countries in Asia and Africa because they can more easily grow enough rice for everyone.

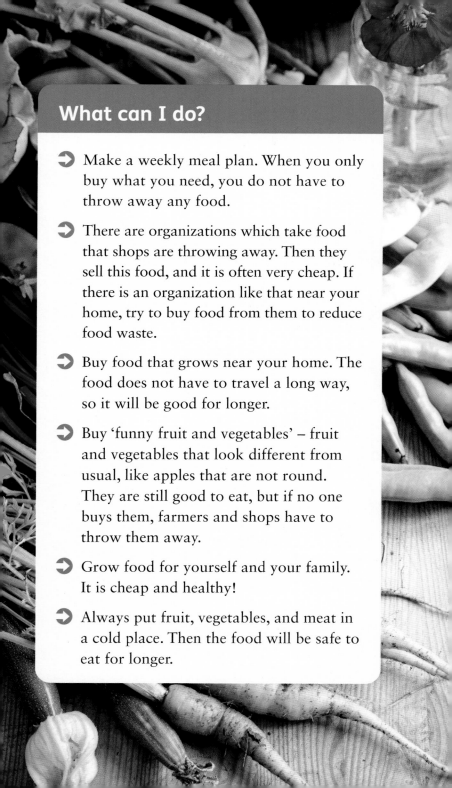

What can I do?

- Make a weekly meal plan. When you only buy what you need, you do not have to throw away any food.

- There are organizations which take food that shops are throwing away. Then they sell this food, and it is often very cheap. If there is an organization like that near your home, try to buy food from them to reduce food waste.

- Buy food that grows near your home. The food does not have to travel a long way, so it will be good for longer.

- Buy 'funny fruit and vegetables' – fruit and vegetables that look different from usual, like apples that are not round. They are still good to eat, but if no one buys them, farmers and shops have to throw them away.

- Grow food for yourself and your family. It is cheap and healthy!

- Always put fruit, vegetables, and meat in a cold place. Then the food will be safe to eat for longer.

4 Good health and clean water

Everyone must have healthy lives.

Everyone must have clean water.

When people are healthy, they can work, live good lives, and care for other people. But there are many people in the world who are ill, have a disease, have a mental health problem, or are badly hurt. Sometimes, people die because they cannot get help from a doctor.

We must have enough health workers and doctors who can give everyone good care when they need it. We must also help people to live safer, healthier lives. For example, everyone must have clean water. People can get very ill when they drink dirty water or when they do not have enough water to wash with, or have clean toilets.

THINK

How much water do you use every day? What do you use it for?

What are the world's biggest health problems?

Every 11 seconds, when a new baby is born, the mother or the baby dies.

1.5 million people die every year because they have not had vaccinations against diseases.

1 in every 4 people will have mental health problems at some time in their lives.

Every year, 1.35 million people die in car crashes.

In many countries in Africa, there are only 10 doctors for every 10,000 people.

In 2019...

2.2 billion people did not have safe drinking water.

4.2 billion people did not have clean toilets.

3 billion people did not have clean water to wash with.

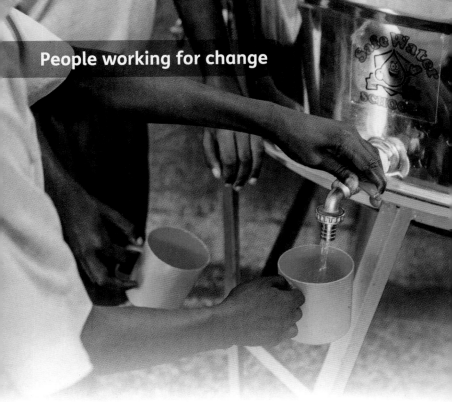

Making clean water in Uganda

In villages in Uganda, people were often ill because the water there was not safe to drink. So, a young man called Timothy Kayondo decided to try and help. He had to find a cheap way to make clean water because many people in these villages are very poor, and they cannot pay a lot of money for water.

Kayondo learned how to clean water with old food waste from meat, fruit, and vegetables. He dries the food waste and uses it to make special water cleaners. When dirty water goes through one of these cleaners, the cleaner takes away any diseases from the water. Schools and health centres in Uganda are beginning to use Kayondo's water cleaners to get clean, safe drinking water.

Helping pregnant women in Nigeria

In just two years, eighteen pregnant women died in the village of Bardo, in the north of Nigeria. The village is thirty kilometres from the nearest hospital, and women could not get there quickly when they had problems with their pregnancies.

A group of women in the village decided to work together to get enough money to buy a car. Now, they have a car and a driver, so when any pregnant woman in the village has a problem with her pregnancy, the driver can take them quickly to the hospital.

What can I do?

- Get your vaccinations, if you can. They are very important because they can stop diseases.

- Always wash your hands after you use the toilet and before you eat, or if your hands are dirty.

- Try to live healthily. Do exercise, spend time outside, eat healthy food, and get enough sleep.

- People should always drive cars carefully, and if you are walking, be careful near roads.

- Help your family and friends to stay healthy and be safe, too. For example, exercise and eat healthy meals together.

5 Education for everyone

Everyone must have a good education and opportunities to learn.

Education is very important because it changes people's lives. For example, when a person has been to school, they can get a good job more easily – so, education reduces poverty and hunger. This is why there must be equality in education: all boys and girls must go to school and have the same opportunities.

In the last ten years, there have been more people in education than before. But in 2018, there were still 260 million children and young people who were not in school. For every four children in the classroom, one child somewhere in the world does not get an education.

THINK

How will your future be better because of your education?

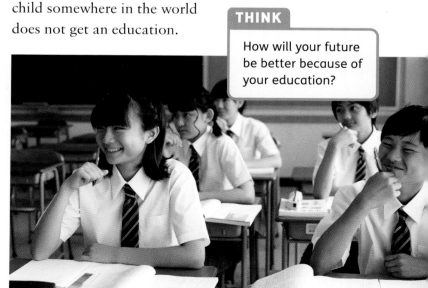

Why are so many young people not in education?

Poverty

- In some countries, there are not many schools or teachers, so children who live too far from a school cannot get there.
- Some children from poor families have to work to get money, so they cannot go to school.
- Some children who are living in poverty cannot walk to school or learn because they are too hungry and tired.

No equality for girls

- Some families only send their boys to school because they think that school is more important for boys, or it is wrong for girls to go to school.
- Sometimes, a school (or the journey to school) is unsafe for girls, so they do not go to school.
- Every year, 12 million girls marry before they are eighteen. Many of these girls have to leave school and start a family.

Bullying

- 1 in every 4 children is bullied while they are in education. Many children who are bullied at school stop going there because they feel too afraid or worried.

Conflict or extreme weather

- Conflict or extreme weather can sometimes destroy schools, so children have nowhere to go to learn.
- Sometimes, families have to leave their homes because it is not safe there, so children have to leave their schools, too.

Health

- About 240 million children have a disability. Nearly half of these children do not go to school because they cannot get the right help to travel to school or learn in a classroom.
- Some parents do not send their children to school because their own lives are very hard. For example, they have a disease or a mental health problem, and they often cannot take their children to school.
- There are thousands of young carers who have to help someone in their family who is very ill. In the UK, about one-quarter of young carers cannot go to school every day.

Giving learning opportunities in Italy

In Italy, new places called 'Punti Luce' (light centres) are helping to bring more equality in education. There are lots of good schools in Italy, and education is free, but the organizations that started the light centres wanted to give more opportunities to children who have difficult home lives, or who live in places without good opportunities. These children can come to the centres and get help with their reading and schoolwork, make friends, play, and learn new things, like music. There are also lessons for mothers and fathers at the light centres, to teach them how to help their children. In just one year, the light centre in Turin has worked with more than 500 children and 200 mothers.

Giving education to Syrian children in Lebanon

Since 2011, 1.5 million people have had to move to Lebanon from Syria to escape the conflict in Syria. These people often have to live without real homes, and their children often cannot travel to Lebanese schools to get an education. Sometimes, the children have seen terrible things in Syria during the conflict, and they need special help to feel safe and ready to learn.

So, an organization called 'Children on the Edge' made a school for Syrian children in Zahlé, in Lebanon. The organization takes children to the school by bus, and they can learn safely there, with Syrian teachers who speak their language and understand their problems.

What can I do?

- Reading is a great way to learn. When you have finished reading a book, give it to a school, or to someone who cannot easily buy books.

- Remember that you are very lucky to have an education. Take every opportunity to learn. If you are still at school, ask your teacher questions or read more about what you are learning. If you have left school, do some free lessons online.

- Help a young person with their homework if you can – or help them with their English!

- Ask what things your school needs, or a school near where you live. Then try and help them to get these things.

6 Equality for women and girls

 5 GENDER EQUALITY

There must be equality in all things for women and girls.

About half the people in the world are women or girls, but many women and girls do not get the same opportunities as men or boys. There is discrimination against women and girls in their communities, in education, at work, and at home, and there is sometimes terrible violence against them, too.

There are also not enough women in important jobs in governments, businesses, and organizations. This is because of discrimination. When women are in important jobs, they can help to give better opportunities to girls and other women. The world will be a better place for everyone when there is real equality for women and girls.

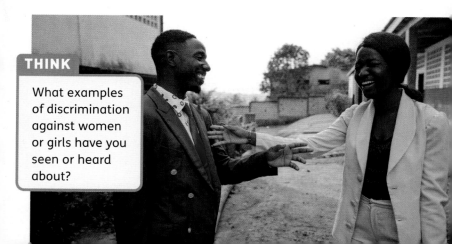

THINK

What examples of discrimination against women or girls have you seen or heard about?

What things are stopping women from having equality?

There is violence against 1 in 3 women and girls at some time in their lives.

Some adults cannot read or write, and nearly two-thirds of these people are women.

In 18 countries, men can tell their wives not to go to work.

In 2019, only 28% of the people in the most important jobs in businesses and organizations were women.

For most jobs, men get 32% more pay than women for the same work.

For every hour that a man does housework, a woman does 2.5 hours.

In 2018, 40% of women in sport said that there has been discrimination against them.

Reducing violence against women in Colombia

Colombia, like a lot of countries in the world, has had a terrible problem with violence against women for many years. For a long time, there have been special phone helplines in Colombia that women can call when they need help because someone has hurt them.

But in December 2020, a new phone helpline started in Colombia – a helpline for men. Men can call 'Linea Calma' when they are feeling angry, and they can talk to people who try to help them. Often, when they have these conversations, the men begin to feel better, and they do not hurt anyone. In the first year of the helpline, nearly 2,000 men called, and people think that it can help to stop violence against women in Colombia.

Helping women to exercise in Türkiye

Sport is very good for your body, and you often feel happier when you exercise, but sometimes women do not feel comfortable at the gym. In Türkiye, men and women do not often exercise together, and many women do not like to use gyms because there are men there. But in 2006, Bedriye Hülya opened some new gyms for women only. Her gyms are cheap and give women a place to feel comfortable when they exercise.

Also, all the people who work in these gyms are women. In Türkiye, only 33% of women work – so the gyms are helping to bring more equality in the workplace, too.

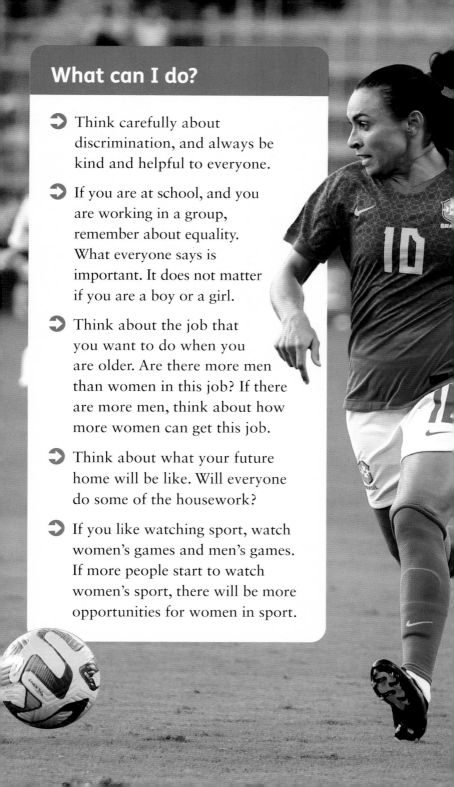

What can I do?

- Think carefully about discrimination, and always be kind and helpful to everyone.

- If you are at school, and you are working in a group, remember about equality. What everyone says is important. It does not matter if you are a boy or a girl.

- Think about the job that you want to do when you are older. Are there more men than women in this job? If there are more men, think about how more women can get this job.

- Think about what your future home will be like. Will everyone do some of the housework?

- If you like watching sport, watch women's games and men's games. If more people start to watch women's sport, there will be more opportunities for women in sport.

7 Good work, economies, and places to live

There must be good work for all adults, and all countries need strong economies.

There must be good businesses and work opportunities for the future.

Everyone must live in good, safe communities.

When an adult works, they can buy what they need for themselves and their family more easily. So, good work opportunities reduce poverty and hunger. Good work makes the country's economy stronger, too, and the government can pay for more things, like schools and roads. So, it is important that there are lots of new and growing businesses that people can work for. Businesses must pay their workers well and everyone needs to be in a safe workplace, with opportunities for all workers to do interesting and new things.

People must also be safe and happy in their homes and communities. In a good community, there are enough homes that are not too expensive, and people can travel around easily by car, bus, or train. Mobile phones and the internet are easy to use, and there are lots of green places with trees and clean air. Good communities have strong buildings and roads, too, so extreme weather cannot destroy them.

THINK

What things does the government pay for in your country? What is your community like?

But in some countries, there are not enough jobs, or there are some jobs, but they are dangerous and do not pay well, and people do not have good places to live.

What are the world's biggest problems at work and at home?

Work

More than 6% of people in the world did not have a job in 2021.

40 million people are in modern slavery. 1 in 4 of these people are children. 71% of them are women or girls. Often, people cannot escape from modern slavery because if they leave, there will be violence against them, and they will have no home or money.

160 million children have to go to work. Because of this, they cannot go to school, play, or do other things that are important for all children.

Every year, around 500 million people are hurt or get diseases in their workplace. 2.3 million of these people die because of what happened to them at work.

Home

150 million people in the world do not have a home.

More than 1 billion people live in slums – places with lots of very small buildings that are unsafe or not healthy.

759 million people do not have lights in their homes. 75% of these people live in countries in Africa.

Nearly 3 billion people have never used the internet. Most of these people live in developing countries, and in many of these countries, nearly 75% of people have never been online.

In many countries in Africa, more than 60% of people cannot travel anywhere because there are no buses or trains near their homes.

Helping people in modern slavery in the US

When people escape from modern slavery, it can be difficult to find a job, so AnnieCannons, a computer business in California, has started teaching these people to build apps and websites. Because they learn something important and useful at AnnieCannons, students can then get good work which pays them well in the future.

Some AnnieCannons students are even building special apps to try and help people. People can use the apps to get help quickly when they are in modern slavery. Because the students who are making these apps understand the problems of modern slavery so well, they are very good at helping to find the answers to them.

Riding safely in Chile

In Santiago, in Chile, there are many cars on the streets, and very bad air pollution, so people cannot go outside and exercise safely in their communities. Because of this, Gonzalo Stierling Aguayo and his wife decided to start 'bicycle Sundays' there. Now, every Sunday until 2 p.m., many roads are only open for bicycles, and people can ride for forty kilometres on roads with no cars. About 40,000 people go out on their bicycles each Sunday and enjoy riding together. Many people think that living in Santiago is much better now because of Stierling Aguayo's 'bicycle Sundays'.

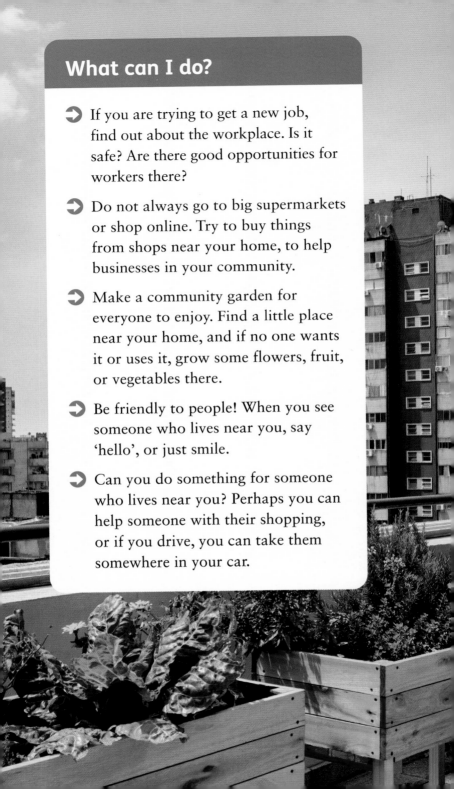

What can I do?

→ If you are trying to get a new job, find out about the workplace. Is it safe? Are there good opportunities for workers there?

→ Do not always go to big supermarkets or shop online. Try to buy things from shops near your home, to help businesses in your community.

→ Make a community garden for everyone to enjoy. Find a little place near your home, and if no one wants it or uses it, grow some flowers, fruit, or vegetables there.

→ Be friendly to people! When you see someone who lives near you, say 'hello', or just smile.

→ Can you do something for someone who lives near you? Perhaps you can help someone with their shopping, or if you drive, you can take them somewhere in your car.

8 An end to climate change

 There must be sustainable energy for everyone.

 We need to make and use things in a sustainable way.

 We must stop climate change.

The Earth is 1°C hotter today than it was 150 years ago, and it is getting hotter. We are already seeing terrible changes in our world because of climate change. There is a lot more extreme weather in some countries, so people cannot grow food, and can lose their homes in fires and storms. If we do not live in a more sustainable way, life on Earth will be very difficult. To end climate change, we need to reduce greenhouse gases. We can do this if we live more sustainably.

THINK

What extreme weather have you had in your country in the last five years?

Where do greenhouse gases come from, and how can we reduce them?

73% MAKING ENERGY

WHAT CAN WE DO?

Countries must use more sustainable energy from the wind, water, and the sun.

Where do greenhouse gases come from?

19% FARMING

WHAT CAN WE DO?

Countries must reduce meat farming and stop destroying trees for farming because trees take greenhouse gases out of the air.

3% WASTE

WHAT CAN WE DO?

People must use things again and recycle them.

5% FACTORIES

WHAT CAN WE DO?

People must stop buying lots of new things that they do not need. Factories must use sustainable energy.

Recycling waste in Brazil

Leandro Neres Abrantes did not like seeing waste on the streets of the slums near his home in Cantagalo, in Rio de Janeiro. He began taking some of the waste away and recycling it. Then, he spoke to the people in his community, and he began recycling some of their waste, too.

Recycling reduces the greenhouse gases that go into the air, and Neres Abrantes's organization Favela+Limpa is now recycling nearly 100,000 kilograms of waste every year. Favela+Limpa's work is also building a better world in other ways. Favela+Limpa gets money when it recycles things, and Neres Abrantes now pays the people who bring their waste to him. This really helps some of the poorest people in his community.

Making sustainable energy in Germany

More than twenty-five years ago, people in Wildpoldsried, in the south of Germany, decided to build a wind farm to make sustainable energy for their town. The wind farm worked very well, so the people there began to make more and more of their energy from the wind, the sun, and water. Now, the town makes all its energy itself – and all the energy is sustainable. And, because it makes more energy than it needs, it can sell a lot of the energy that it makes to other towns. Wildpoldsried has used the money to build a new school and other good things in the town.

What can I do?

- For short journeys, ride a bicycle or walk, and do not go by car.

- For long journeys, try to travel by train or boat, and not on a plane, because planes put a lot of greenhouse gases into the air.

- Stop eating meat, or try to only eat meat once or twice a week. If, for every three meals, everyone only eats meat in one of them, we can reduce the greenhouse gases in the air by 60%.

- Turn off lights when you are not in a room, and do not make your house so warm in the winter if you do not need to.

- If you have a garden, grow a tree. Trees take greenhouse gases out of the air.

- Only buy things when you really need them, and when you do not want something, do not throw it away. Give it to someone who needs it.

- Do not always buy things that are new. You can buy lots of good things from shops that sell other people's old things.

- When you use glass, plastic, or paper, try to use it again and again. If you cannot, always recycle it.

9   A healthier Earth

 14 LIFE BELOW WATER   We must care for our oceans and everything in them.

 15 LIFE ON LAND   We must care for the land and all the plants and animals that live on it.

Earth is our home, and it is the home of every animal and plant, too. But many plants and animals are going extinct because we are not caring well enough for the oceans and the land. This is terrible for animals and plants, and it is bad for people, too, because we cannot live without the plants and animals on Earth. We must change how we live, and how we care for the oceans, to give all living things in our world a good, safe future.

THINK

What animals in your country are going extinct? Do you know why they are going extinct?

Why are plants and animals in danger?

Every year, billions of kilograms of plastic waste go into the oceans, killing millions of animals.

Pollution from farming and factories goes into the land, rivers, and oceans, and pollution from boats goes into the oceans, too.

Climate change is killing many ocean animals and plants that cannot live in warmer waters. Extreme weather and fires are killing many land animals, too.

About 4 million boats catch fish from our oceans every day, and because of this, some fish and other sea animals are going extinct.

Forests and wetlands are the homes of many plants and animals, but every day, people are destroying them to build new farms and houses. We are destroying more than 15 billion trees every year.

Many of the world's wild animals are also going extinct because people kill them for meat, or people catch the wild animals to sell them.

Catching fish in Mexico

When boats catch a lot of fish, they do not just catch what they want. Often, they also catch sea animals or big fish that are in danger of going extinct. These animals sometimes die or are badly hurt. But, some people in Mexico have found a good answer to this problem. Because these sea animals can see green light very well, some fishing boats there are now using green lights. The sea animals and big fish see the green lights and they swim away from them, and the green lights have reduced the number of sea animals which are dying in this way by 63%.

Planting a forest in India

When Jadav Payeng was twenty years old, he saw dead animals on an island in the Brahmaputra River near his home, in India. There were no trees on the island to keep the animals safe from the hot sun, so the animals died. Payeng decided to plant a forest on the island. In 1979, he began going to the island every day to plant trees. And, slowly, he made a forest.

Today, the forest is bigger than Central Park, in New York City, in the US, and many different animals and plants live there. Payeng's forest, which is now called the Molai Forest, is also helping with the problem of climate change because trees take greenhouse gases out of the air. In 2010, the Indian government gave Payeng the name 'The Forest Man of India', and he now works with other countries around the world to help their forests, too.

Jadav Payeng

What can I do?

- Do not get thin, plastic bags when you go shopping. Buy strong bags and use them again and again.

- Try not to buy things in plastic boxes. If you need to use plastic boxes, do not throw them away. Keep them and use them again.

- Do not buy water or drinks in plastic bottles and cups. Get a bottle and a cup that you can put drinks in again and again.

- Read what it says on the bags or boxes of food that you buy. If people make or grow food in a sustainable way, it is better for our world. Try to buy this food.

- Help with town, village, or beach cleaning days in your community.

- Reduce how much paper you use. Work on a computer when you can, and use both sides of every piece of paper.

- If you have a garden, learn how to grow things in a way that is good for the animals and plants in your garden.

10 No conflict or violence

Everyone must be safe from violence and conflict.

We all want to feel safe and live freely, but often there is conflict between people, groups, or countries. When there is conflict, many people die, and people cannot live or work safely. In 2020, 25% of people were living in countries that were in conflict.

All around the world there is violent crime, too. Nearly 500,000 people died from violent crimes in 2017 – and more than 30% of people, most of them women, are afraid to walk outside at night.

Many people also feel unsafe in their communities, schools, or workplaces because there is bullying or discrimination. But we must all be free to live without conflict or violence.

THINK

Where is there conflict in the world right now? Do you know why the conflict is happening?

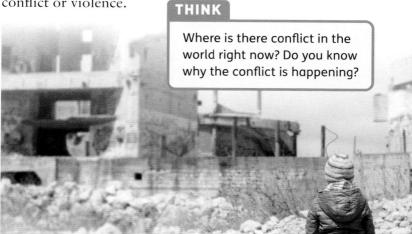

What happens in a country that is working to stop conflict and violence?

Everyone lives freely and has the same opportunities. It does not matter what they look like, or what they think.

Everyone knows that they cannot hurt other people or steal anything.

The government and the police work hard to end violent crime, discrimination, and bullying.

The government works with other governments all around the world to end conflict and violence.

The people of the country decide all the important things that happen in their lives, and they decide who works in their government.

People with important jobs in government are good, and do things because they care about their country and its people.

Bringing students together in Kenya

In West Pokot, in Kenya, there was often conflict between Kenyan people and people from Uganda because people from both countries needed water and land for their cows, and there was not enough for everyone. Hundreds of people died fighting, and many had to leave their homes.

But in 2019, Katikomor School was built there to teach children from Kenya and Uganda. The school brings together students from these different places and teaches them to understand how other people live. The students at Katikomor School are now friends, and are helping to build a new future without conflict and violence between their countries.

Learning from babies in Canada

In schools in Canada, teachers wanted to find a way to stop bullying, so mothers and fathers are now bringing their babies to schools to help with special classes there. The students in these classes watch a baby play. They can see when the baby is happy, and when it is unhappy.

Teachers say that these classes are teaching their students an important lesson: we are all people and we all feel the same things, so we must be kind and caring to everyone.

Teachers are seeing a lot of changes in their students because of the lessons, and they now know that these classes are reducing bullying in schools.

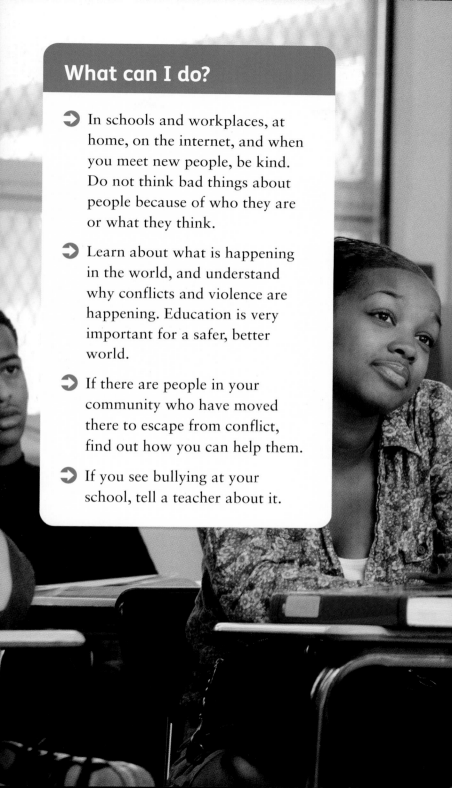

What can I do?

➡ In schools and workplaces, at home, on the internet, and when you meet new people, be kind. Do not think bad things about people because of who they are or what they think.

➡ Learn about what is happening in the world, and understand why conflicts and violence are happening. Education is very important for a safer, better world.

➡ If there are people in your community who have moved there to escape from conflict, find out how you can help them.

➡ If you see bullying at your school, tell a teacher about it.

11 Into the future

17 PARTNERSHIPS FOR THE GOALS — Countries must work together and help developing countries.

The last goal of the SDGs, SDG 17, calls for countries to work together on the changes that must happen in our world. When countries work together, they can do a lot more than they can alone. This is true for people, groups, and organizations, too.

Every year, the UN looks at how much each country has done for the different SDGs. A lot of wonderful things are happening, but change is not happening fast enough, and we must all do a lot more. There is still time – and you do not need to work for a government or a big organization to do useful things. When we change our lives, even in the smallest ways, and explain what we are doing and why, we are helping our world.

Mahatma Gandhi, the great Indian thinker, once said that *if we can change ourselves, then the world will change, too*. Let's make a change, every one of us, and build a better world!

Mahatma Gandhi

climate *(n)* the usual weather in a place

conflict *(n)* when people, groups, or countries do not agree, and they are fighting

economy *(n)* how a country spends its money and makes, buys, and sells things

education *(n)* the teaching of a person, for example, at school

equality *(n)* when everyone has the same opportunities

health *(n)* when someone has good health, they are not ill; **healthy** *(adj)* not ill

hunger *(n)* not having enough food to eat

poverty *(n)* when someone is very poor

air *(n)* the space around and above things

bullying *(n)* when someone hurts another person who is not as strong as them, again and again

care *(n & v)* to help someone or something so they feel or are better

clean *(adj)* not dirty

community *(n)* all the people who live in a place together

destroy *(v)* to break or stop something

disability *(n)* when someone cannot use a part of their body well or easily, or cannot learn easily

discrimination *(n)* when people are unkind to another person, or to a group of people, because they are different to them; when a group of people do not have the same opportunities as other groups

disease *(n)* an illness; often you get it from another person

Earth *(n)* this world; the planet that we live on

energy *(n)* We need energy for lots of things, like watching television, cooking, and driving a car.

enough *(det)* as many or as much as somebody needs or wants

exercise *(n & v)* moving your body; exercise makes you stronger and healthier

(go) extinct *(adj)* If an animal or plant goes extinct, there are no more of that animal or plant on Earth.

extreme *(adj)* very much

farm *(n)* people keep animals for meat or milk, and grow food on a farm

forest *(n)* a place that has lots of trees in it

future *(n)* a time that will come, e.g. tomorrow, next week, etc.

goal *(n)* something that you hope to do in the future

government *(n)* the people who decide important things for a country

greenhouse gas *(n)* one of the gases around the Earth that keeps the Earth warm

grow *(v)* when something grows, it gets bigger

gym *(n)* a room or building where people do exercise

land *(n)* the part of the Earth that is not the ocean

mental health *(n)* the way that someone thinks and feels about themselves and the world; when someone has good mental health, they feel happy and enjoy life

modern slavery *(n)* When someone is in modern slavery, other people tell them to do bad or dangerous work for no money, or only a little money.

ocean *(n)* the salt water over most of the Earth

opportunity *(n)* You have an opportunity when it is possible for you to do something.

organization *(n)* a group of people who work together

plant *(n)* a tree, flower, vegetable, etc. that grows from the ground; **plant** *(v)* to put things in the ground to grow

plastic *(n & adj)* We use plastic to make lots of things, like plastic bottles and plastic bags.

pollution *(n)* when water, like the sea or a river, the air, or the ground is dirty because of something that people have done

pregnant *(adj)* when a woman has a baby that is growing inside her; **pregnancy** *(n)* the time when a woman is pregnant

problem *(n)* something that is difficult; something that you worry about

recycle *(v)* to make new things from the things people throw away; **recycling** *(n)* when the things that you throw away are made into new things so people can use them again

reduce *(v)* when something gets smaller

safe *(adj)* not in any danger

sustainable *(adj)* when we make things in a way that does not hurt our Earth

throw away *(phr v)* when you do not keep something because you do not want it any more

vaccination *(n)* When a doctor or nurse gives you a vaccination for a disease, your body learns to stop that disease so you do not get very ill from it.

violence *(n)* when someone tries to hurt or kill somebody; **violent** *(adj)* If a person is violent, they hurt other people.

waste *(n)* things that no one wants or needs any more

Think Ahead

1 Read the back cover of the book. Answer the questions.

1 How many countries are in the United Nations?

2 What did these countries agree on?

3 What are the three big problems in the world that are given on the back cover?

4 What must we do to build a better world?

2 Here are three more big problems in the world. Do you think these problems are important? Why / Why not?

1 There is inequality between people (everyone does not have the same rights and opportunities).

2 Many of the animals in the world, on land, and in the sea, are not safe. They do not have good places to live or enough food to eat.

3 Not all children can go to school safely or easily, and they do not get a good education.

3 RESEARCH Now, choose one of the problems in exercise 2 and find the answers to these questions.

1 Is this a problem in your country? Find numbers to show if this is or is not a problem in your country.

2 What organizations are there in your country that are working to end this problem?

3 What can you do to help end this problem?

Chapter Check

CHAPTER 1 Choose the correct words.

1 The SDGs were agreed in *2015 / 2020*.

2 There are *seventeen / nineteen* SDGs.

3 SDG 10 talks about *equality / climate change*.

4 When we live in a sustainable way, it is *safe / dangerous* for the future of our world.

5 Problems like poverty and hunger got *better / worse* after 2019 because of Covid-19.

6 We *help / do not help* our world when we only make small changes.

CHAPTER 2 Are the sentences true or false?

1 The word *poverty* means 'having too much money'.

2 When someone does not have more than $1.90 a day, they are living in extreme poverty.

3 20% of children in the world live in extreme poverty.

4 It is easy to escape from poverty.

5 Wyson Lungu sells milk to people in villages in Nigeria.

6 Tenohasi, in Tokyo, helps people who do not have homes.

CHAPTER 3 Why is there so much hunger in the world? Tick (✓) five things.

a ☐ climate change   e ☐ more people

b ☐ conflict   f ☐ special dryers

c ☐ Green Super Rice   g ☐ food waste

d ☐ poverty   h ☐ equality

CHAPTER 4 Match the sentence halves.

1 Sometimes, people cannot get help...

2 People must have enough clean water...

3 1.35 million people are killed...

4 1.5 million people die every year...

a in car crashes every year.

b because they have not had vaccinations.

c from a doctor.

d to drink and to wash with.

CHAPTER 5 Complete the sentences with the correct adjectives.

afraid   dangerous   extreme   same   tired

1 Everyone must have the _____ opportunities in education.

2 Some poor children cannot get to school because they are too _____.

3 Sometimes, girls cannot go to school because it is too _____.

4 Conflict or _____ weather can destroy schools, and children have nowhere to go to learn.

5 Children who are bullied can feel _____ to learn.

CHAPTER 6 Where is there discrimination against women and girls? Complete the words.

1 w___ k   2 e_____ n

3 h___ e   4 g_____ s

5 s____ t   6 b_____ s

CHAPTER 7 Answer the questions with the words below.

40 million   500 million   759 million   1 billion   3 billion

How many people…

1 are in modern slavery?

2 are hurt or get diseases in their workplace every year?

3 live in slums?

4 do not have lights in their homes?

5 have never used the internet?

CHAPTER 8 Correct the <u>underlined</u> words.

1 The Earth is already 1°C <u>colder</u> than it was 150 years ago.

2 There are more big <u>farms</u> because of climate change.

3 To stop climate change, we must use <u>more</u> greenhouse gases.

4 19% of greenhouses gases come from <u>waste</u>.

5 Favela+Limpa <u>makes</u> nearly 100,000 kilograms of waste every year.

6 The people in Wildpoldsried built a <u>factory</u> to make energy for their town.

CHAPTER 9 Tick (✓) the two sentences which are true.

1 Millions of kilograms of plastic waste go into the sea every year.   ☐

2 Many ocean animals are dying because the sea is too warm for them now.   ☐

3 People are destroying forests and wetlands to build new houses and farms.   ☐

4 Many of the world's wild animals are going
   extinct because other animals are killing them. ☐

5 Boats in Mexico use blue lights to help sea animals. ☐

CHAPTER 10 Complete each sentence with one word from
the text.

1 One quarter of people were living in countries in
   c_____ in 2020.

2 People must live freely and have the same o_____.

3 People must not h_____ other people.

4 The police and government must work to end
   v_____ crime.

5 People must d_____ who works in their own
   country's government.

ALL CHAPTERS Write the number of each SDG.

a Education for everyone

b Good job opportunities

c Equality in and between countries

d Countries work together

e Equality for women and girls

f Living in a sustainable way

g Clean water for everyone

h Caring for our oceans

i Caring for the land

j Sustainable energy

k No conflict or violence

l No poverty

Focus on Vocabulary

1 Match the words with the definitions.

1 conflict   4 health

2 education   5 hunger

3 equality   6 poverty

a the teaching of a person, for example, at school

b not having enough food to eat

c how well or ill someone is

d when everyone has the same opportunities

e when people, groups, or countries are fighting

f when someone is very poor

2 Complete the sentences with the correct adjectives.

clean   extinct   extreme   sustainable   violent

1 People must have _____ water to drink and to wash with, or they will be ill.

2 _____ crime is a terrible problem because people are hurt or killed.

3 Because of climate change, there is more _____ weather and it can be difficult to grow enough food.

4 Every year, more fish go _____ because people catch too many of them.

5 We must make changes in a _____ way, or we will make bigger problems for the future.

Focus on Language

1 Complete the sentences using the past continuous.

1 Bad weather _____ (destroy) rice fields in China.

2 Some men in Colombia _____ (feel) angry before they called the helpline 'Linea Calma'.

3 Women _____ (not exercise) in gyms in Türkiye.

4 More than 6% of people _____ (not work) in 2021.

5 Leandro Neres Abrantes _____ (recycle) the waste on the streets near his home in Rio de Janeiro.

2 DECODE Read the text from Chapter 3. What are *who* and *which* giving information about?

> They pay women [1]who live in the villages of Maharashtra to dry fruit and vegetables, [2]which are then good to eat for up to six months.

a fruit and vegetables   b women

3 DECODE Now, read these sentences and underline *which* and *who*. Then match the words to when we use them.

> There are organizations which take food that shops are throwing away.

> There are thousands of young carers who have to help someone in their family who is very ill.

1 *who*   a is used to talk about things

2 *which*   b is used to talk about people

Discussion

1 **Read the sentences giving ideas. Which world problem are the speakers trying to end? How will each of the ideas help to end this problem?**

A: <u>How about</u> we plant a tree in the garden?

B: <u>Shall we</u> go on holiday by boat, and not on a plane?

C: <u>Let's</u> ride our bicycles to the shops, and not go by car.

D: <u>Why don't we</u> stop eating meat?

E: <u>What about</u> the lights in the house? We must turn them off when we are not in a room.

2 **Think of two more ideas that will help to end one of the world problems in exercise 1. Use the <u>underlined</u> words in exercise 1 to give you ideas.**

3 **THINK CRITICALLY** **Now, choose a different world problem in this book. Give five ideas for things that you can do to end this problem. Use the <u>underlined</u> words in exercise 1, and the 'What can I do?' pages in each chapter to help you.**

4 **COMMUNICATE** **Take turns to read your ideas in exercise 3 to a partner. Choose one idea each that you want to start to do in your life, and answer the questions.**

1 Why did you choose this idea?

2 Why is it important, do you think?

3 When will you start?

4 Where will you do it?

5 Who will you tell about it?

1 **Choose one of the 'People working for change' pages in this book and answer the questions.**

  1 What is the person's and / or organization's name?

  2 Where is the person and / or organization?

  3 What was the problem that the person or organization was trying to end?

  4 What did the person or organization do? Was it easy or difficult?

  5 How have they changed people's lives, do you think?

2 **Now, find out about a person or organization who is working for change in your town or city, or in your country. Answer the questions in exercise 1 about the person or organization.**

3 **CREATE Use your answers in exercise 2 to write a paragraph for the SDG website about the person or organization. Use the 'People working for change' pages in this book to help you. Draw pictures with your paragraph.**

4 **COMMUNICATE Read a partner's paragraph. Can you answer the questions in exercise 1 using your partner's paragraph?**

RACHEL BLADON

1969–2022

Author and Series Editor

This is the last book Rachel Bladon wrote for *Oxford Bookworms Library*. She was a wonderful author and Series Editor, and her books won many prizes. She wanted to tell the best stories possible for readers of all ages. Important ideas in her books are: equality for women and girls; the animal world and sustainability; adventure; being kind and friendly; mental health and well-being. Rachel thought that reading is a great way to learn English, and also to learn about life.

Rachel also did lots of things in her community. In the early days of Covid-19, she started a 'help-your-neighbour' group, and also gave vaccinations. In 2022, she taught English to Ukrainian families who escaped from conflict. These and very many other 'small changes' were her big way of building a better world.

Audio Download

Level 2

Building a Better World

You can activate your code only once.

❶ Go to **www.oup.com/elt/download**

❷ Enter your access code. Follow the instructions on screen.

Need help? Email Customer Support at **eltsupport@oup.com**

OXFORD
UNIVERSITY PRESS

ISBN 978-0-19-426796-0

9 780194 267960